Breathe

A PASTOR'S JOURNEY TO WHOLENESS

"But Jesus often withdrew to lonely places and prayed."
Luke: 5:16

Printed in the United States of America

ISBN: 978-1-7357616-0-2

Kingdomboss Publishing

Thank you!

I want to thank God for calling me into ministry,
a place where I do not feel worthy to serve, but only by God's
grace and mercy do I serve.

I thank my mother for her love, support, and prayers. Your love
is immeasurable.

I thank my husband for the sacrifice he made to travel with me
on this journey, for his "YES" to leaving our home church and
following where God was leading me.

I thank God for my daughter, for the times when I was young in
ministry and used her as sermon illustrations. I had no idea how
embarrassed she was. Thank God we can now laugh.
Love you one, two, three, and more…

I thank God for the first church I served, John Wesley United
Methodist Church. Together we walked through what was one of
the most challenging times as pastor and congregation.

I thank Dr. Deborah Haskins for encouraging me to slow down.
A pastor's wife, she understood the stress ministry can have on
the body. Even during her challenges, she found time to remind
me to take care of myself.

I dedicate this book to the late Rev. Dr. Bruce Franklin Haskins,
who taught me how to embrace the position to which God had
called me. His favorite saying was, "You got this, Prioleau!"
Thanks, Pastor Haskins!

To my colleagues in ministry, **BREATHE!**

Table of Contents

FOREWORD

First, it is an honor and a privilege for me to write this foreword in Rev. Twanda Prioleau's amazing book, written by my pastor from the heart and first-hand knowledge of the impact of clergy burnout and self-care challenges. Pastor Prioleau is truly a pastor! My husband stated, "I look forward to you becoming my pastor," as he transitioned from full-time ministry to disability leave due to a major health crisis and significant health challenges.

As the spouse of an amazing pastoral leader (Rev. Dr. Bruce F. Haskins), and also as a licensed clinical professional counselor, addictions specialist/leader, and retired tenured counselor educator, I know *both* personally and professionally from my over 30 years of clinical experience supporting mental health wellness in the community, and especially among diverse cultural communities (especially supporting faith/spiritual communities), of the negative impacts on mental health, including burnout.

My personal experience includes journeying with my husband during his almost 33 years of ministry before his death (in 2016). When I said, "I Do" to God and to Bruce, I had no idea what ministry would be!!! I only knew that I loved my husband, and I loved the Lord! It was just that simple. I did not need much else. Together we worked as a team; we supported each other personally, spiritually, psychologically, cognitively, and physically. Unlike many 2nd career ministers, ministry couples, and ministry families,

1

I knew at the start that ministry is more than full-time; but even then, I did not fully appreciate the demands. Ministry is 24/7; but, I still had no clue what life would really be like.

Research documents (Visker, Rider, & Humphers-Ginther, 2017) that a large percentage of workers experience stress, which is the precursor to occupational burnout. Persons working in "human services" professions may experience higher levels even more (Maslach, 2003, p. 189), and in so many other ways. Visker et al., 2017 further notes that clergy members, who are not only responsible for fulfilling their spiritual responsibilities as the head of a congregation, are also often called on for a variety of other duties necessary for the well-being of the general public. Some of these duties include supporting the community experiencing community-level trauma from homicidal loss, advocacy for social injustice (i.e., police brutality), and a host of other outside-the-typical clergy job description. These authors also document that a variety of both intrapersonal and external factors associated with higher levels of burnout has been identified, such as "lack of control, unclear job expectations, dysfunctional workplace dynamics, mismatch in values, poor job fit, extremes in activities, lack of social support (i.e., friendship networks may not understand that the pastor cannot opt-out of activities, a spouse, loved one, family member wants/needs the clergy member more and unable to "negotiate" family needs/demands/expectations) and work-life imbalance." (Mayo Clinic, 2015, para. 4). Further, research also reports risk factors related to burnout among clergy members, specifically including "loneliness and isolation" (Scott & Lovell 2015, p. 91).

I know from our ministry life together that the research reports are real! I watched my husband and other clergy colleagues and their families often struggle with the imbalance of work-life. Even when a clergy member goes on vacation, the needs continue: people die, and often the family wants "their" pastor no matter what. While these needs are understandable, what is also real is that clergy are human beings with hearts, minds, spirits, and families that deserve attention, including balanced self-care. What does clergy and family self-care look like? Many clergy do not understand what self-care actually is. I recall in our early years of marriage Bruce who was an amazing leader, church administrator, pastor, and preacher work until the wee hours. It was typical for the children and I to turn in first, and he was still "grinding." In "regular" jobs, there are some occupations that are "exempt" from overtime while there are many where beyond the expected job schedule, one is compensated for overtime/comp time. Well, God, we know, keeps track of ministry commitment, efforts and that the rewards are provided by him and in Heaven. But as my husband often preached, and I "preach" to my mental wellness clients and communities, it is also vital that we have joy here on earth! What are the threats to joy for clergy and their families? These threats include the constant demands on time and the inability of congregations and community members to understand that clergy (and their families) also need balance. God expects us to live a balanced life. Even He got tired, Jesus got tired and said, "I need a break… I'm going to go off to myself and take some time to be still and rest."

Rev. Twanda Prioleau has written this self-care reflective book that is so profoundly genuine, authentic, and a completely honest narrative of the challenges she faced in ministry and other clergy also faced. What is heartfelt is that she shares that the pastor is HUMAN! You live, breathe, and experience life just like all persons: the people you are ministering to and leading. But she shares the heart and gut-wrenching reality that pastors do not "get a pass." They often do not acquire normative time to journey through transitions, including losses. What happens when the pastor experiences life? Are they supposed to just prioritize others over their own always? This reflective book underscores the importance of making my own self-care as a human and clergy leader; emphasizes that our families' self-care is a priority also.

FOREWORD

I loved this book. This book touched me on a personal level after watching my husband and others. I watched them experience losses just as we had and developmental life experiences. I always prayed for my husband, with my husband, and we prayed and prioritized time for our children. I am grateful that he and we would "steal away" for family night on Fridays, taking the children to the park, to get ice cream, and on family vacations (often to visit my mother out of town which was free!). My hope for every clergy person reading this book is that you will read and *commit to your self-care and the self-care of your family!* Because what will sustain us when it is all done, is not that we worked one extra hour (because in reality, we will never catch up!). It is that while we were making disciples of Jesus Christ that we also modeled for ourselves, families, and communities the model that God and Jesus Christ gave us. Self-care and balance are essential. It is not selfish to take time for self. Self-care is the ultimate honoring of the scripture, "Do you not know that your bodies are temples of the Holy Spirit, who is in you, whom you have received from God? You are not your own; you were brought at a price. Therefore, honor God with your bodies (1 Corinthians 6:19-20 NIV). Amen.

Dr. Deborah G. Haskins
Licensed Clinical Professional Counselor
Master Addiction Counselor
Owner/Chief Clinical Consultant
MOSAIC Consulting and Counseling Services
July, 2020

BREATHE!

Have you ever felt like you were holding your breath in life, and if you let it go, you might drown? Ministry can make you feel like you are holding your breath, waiting to breathe. We encounter one event after another. One emergency after another waiting to be relieved of our constantly, ever-moving life. We are breathing in the cares of this world, one news report after another. We are breathing in the rapid changes in our society. Can we really keep up? We are breathing in the concerns and constant reports of family emergencies in our congregations. Let's not forgot the community needs our attention. We are connecting with schools, businesses, organizations, civil groups and other faith communities. Can our church survive the constant changes in our neighborhood? We are breathing in statistical reports. Will the numbers add up? Is the congregation growing numerically? Those of us that serve in Methodist denominations are breathing in the apportionments. Can the church make ends meet? *Have you ever felt like you were holding your breath?* We breathe in being accepted by a new congregation. Will the people like me? I know I am not the previous pastor. We are breathing in a lot, but we are always holding our breath. We need to give ourselves permission to let things go and allow God to take the burden of ministry.

BREATHE!

Yes, serving in ministry is a blessing. However, life in ministry can also be a burden, and some of us hold the weight of ministry in too long. Exhale! When we exhale, we allow God to breathe for us. When we exhale, we speak truth to ourselves and admit that we are leading from an empty cup. When we exhale, we are reminded that our cup only overflows when we allow God to pour into that cup. When we exhale, We. Slow. Down. Enough. To. Hear. God's. Still. Small. Voice. **BREATHE!**

Why I share my story...

I share my story because I understand that many of us (clergy) are reluctant to express how we REALLY feel. I believe many of us are afraid to say we are tired. We are scared to say we are depressed and weighted down with the cares of this world. We are scared to say we are not doing well spiritually, and there are times when we don't feel God's presence. We are so afraid because of what we think others might say. People might think we are operating out of little faith or no faith. I understand because I lived it. I know how you are feeling. I have experienced the ups and downs of ministry. I understand how clergy sometimes feel as though we don't have an outlet. I understand that there are times when we feel like we have no one with whom to talk. I know that ministry comes with joys, but it also comes with sorrows. Sorrows that some will never be able to understand. I understand. I believe we feel this way because clergy are criticized and scrutinized daily. We live our lives in a fishbowl and under a microscope. So, what do we say? ALL IS WELL. We say this even when all is not well.

After serving seven years in full-time ministry, I suffered clergy burnout. I found myself depleted and void of things that would bring joy to my life. I felt empty inside. I had lost my zeal for ministry. Ministry was not bringing me joy anymore. It was draining. I was mentally, physically, and spiritually tired. At that time, I felt like I had two options, either I step away from ministry for a period or quit. Thank God I chose to step away for a period. Eventually, I took a three-month sabbath leave.

After stepping back, I learned to BREATHE. "But Jesus often withdrew to lonely places and prayed." Luke: 5:16 (NIV) I had to learn to withdraw to lonely places of silence and solitude and BREATHE. Today, I am determined to just BE- be the best that I can be and allow God to do the rest. Live in the moment. Be in the moment. Feel the moment. Embrace the moment. BREATHE!

Most of what you read in this book I wrote during my sabbath leave. It's incredible how we can hear clearly from God when we step back and sit in silence. Just you and God!

Maybe you are tired, worn-out, and not sure what's happening. Perhaps you feel depleted and don't have the words to articulate how you are feeling. I share my story in hopes that it gives voice to what you are experiencing and allows you to give yourself permission to BREATHE! There is a peace that only comes from being in the presence of God.

1

NEW TERRITORY

In 2007, sensing a call to pastoral ministry, I took a leap of faith and entered seminary. I was both baptized as a young girl and ordained clergy in the Baptist denomination. However, it was in seminary that I fell in love with the United Methodist emphasis on grace. It filled some gaps in my theology, especially as it pertains to infant baptism and the sacraments. In 2009, while in seminary, I sensed a call to leave the Baptist denomination. I joined the United Methodist Church. Knowing that the decision I was making would have an impact on my family, it was not an easy move. I was asking my husband to leave the denomination in which he grew up and had been ordained a deacon, and follow the path God was leading me to.

I did not know how things would unfold, but I was trusting God. I can only imagine what he was going through and what he was feeling at the time. I remember the hesitancy he expressed the first time I shared with him that God was leading me to pastor in the United Methodist Church. It was not an easy decision for either of us. We both would be leaving the denomination in which we grew up. Most of our family are Baptist. It felt like I was leaving my family and friends behind. Some people who do not understand the concept of denominations asked if I was separating from the faith. At the time, we had been serving together in youth ministry. Connecting with a new ministry would be a major shift in our lives.

To be honest, I pondered a lot of questions, especially for my marriage. How would a new church have an impact on us? I am a woman in ministry, and it's not easy. What are the sacrifices of pastoral ministry? I did not know. What would change? I did not know. How would things change? No longer would we be strategizing and planning ministry together. What about my daughter? At the time she was 17 years old. Would I ask her to move churches with us? I had heard about the sacrifice of pastoral ministry, the stress it could have on pastors and their families, and I was a little scared. I was walking in uncharted territory. But as I moved forward, I held onto something God ministered to me when I was in seminary, and that was "Trust God in the process."

Let me tell you a story.

In January 2009, I had an opportunity to travel to Egypt. While in Egypt, I had the chance to climb Mt. Sinai. I remember the climb as if it were yesterday. The date was Monday, January 12, 2009, and we arrived late in the evening at St. Catherine's Monastery, which is at the foot of Mt. Sinai. Arriving at the foot of Mt. Sinai, already tired from the events of that day and a long bus ride, we had to eat dinner and retire for the night. Our climb up the mountain would start at 2 a.m. the next morning. We were told to layer our clothes and bring a flashlight for the climb. So, we start this walk-up Mt. Sinai. It was cold, dark, and the temperatures would drop even further the higher we climbed. In the beginning, I was excited. In my limited imagination, I imagined the walk that Moses walked. Immediately it became a spiritual journey for me.

Interestingly, I was surprised that the trail started uphill. I was even more astonished that shortly into the walk, I began to feel tired. I am sure we were only 10 to 15 minutes into a four-hour walk when I felt like I was not going to make it to the top of the mountain. I am sure some of those who were traveling with me would say it was less because they had to stop and wait for me twice. Eventually, I gave in to taking a camel ride up the mountain. I was so afraid to get on that camel, but I wanted so bad to make it to the top. Those who were with me encouraged me as I mounted the camel, assuring me we would meet at some point during the journey. Immediately, after climbing the camel, fear set in. This animal was not only massive but tall, and I have a fear of heights.

I was so afraid. It was dark and cold, and there were times when the camel appeared to be walking on what seemed to be the edge of the mountain. Also, I was placed on the lead camel, and he walked up this mountain with no human assistance. Oh how I prayed! I relied on the encouragement of my classmates to carry me through this ride that seemed like it would never end. I had two choices; I could stay on this camel, or I could turn around and abort the trip. In order to continue, I had to trust and believe that God was with me. I had to trust and believe that although I was riding on a camel, it was God that was going to protect me. To get to the top of the mountain, I had to take my trust out of the ability of the camel and place that trust in God. As if the camel ride was not enough, about two-thirds of the way up the mountain, the camel stopped, and I had to climb the rest. I felt like I was back at the beginning attempting to climb the mountain for the first time. Now, as I began to climb again with the group, I had to rely on the physical strength of others while depending on spiritual strength from God. But when we reached the top of that mountain, oh what joy filled my soul! We had finally reached our destination! Out of the darkness, into the light. The joy of the sunrise on that mountaintop was so moving. We sang and prayed. We rejoiced and gave God praise. All the fear I had as we climbed up that mountain disappeared. Once we returned to our bus, I heard these words. "Trust God in the process." I held onto these words. I shared that story because throughout my process, God continued to take me back to that experience and those words.

2
GOD'S PROCESS

*"But the Lord said to Samuel, "Do not consider his
appearance or his height, for I have rejected him. The Lord
does not look at the things people look at. People look at the outward
appearance, but the Lord looks at the heart."
1 Samuel 16:7 (NIV)*

July 1, 2011, I entered pastoral ministry as the Associate
Pastor of John Wesley United Methodist Church in
Baltimore City. I would be serving with The Reverend Dr.
Bruce Franklin Haskins, who had been appointed at the same
time as the senior pastor. Pastor Haskins had been serving as
a pastor in the United Methodist Church for over 30 years.
On the same day, at midnight to be exact, this historic
congregation received a pastor with three decades of
experience and a pastor for whom this was day one on the
job. In the United Methodist Church, we are itinerant
pastors. "United Methodist pastors are sent, not called or
hired. 'Itinerancy' refers specifically to the commitment of
pastors to go and serve wherever the Resident Bishop sends
them." This means we can oversee a church and, after a year
or so, be assigned to serve another congregation. I had no
idea what was in store for me. He had 30 years of ministry

experience, and I was just starting my pastoral ministry with no prior pastoral experience.

It was one of the best days of my life. However, I felt like I was way out of my comfort zone. The feeling when God calls you to do something, and you are saying, "Who me?" That is how I felt. It was my first time serving as a pastor, I was new to the United Methodist Church, and many people in this denomination did not know me.

However, it amazes me how God works in our lives. If everything had gone according to man's plans, I would have never been chosen to be the new associate pastor of John Wesley United Methodist Church. The Baltimore-Washington Conference had a process in place to select an associate pastor for this church. However, after the plans did not work, God's perfect plan for my life took place. I had just finished a unit of Clinical Pastoral Education at York County Hospital. I accepted a position as a chaplain intern for a year when I received a call on a Friday in March 2011 from the then District Superintendent asking me to consider taking a pastoral position at a church in Baltimore City. I said, "Yes." He shared with me that he would call me back on Monday with the details. I had no idea what church it was.

I was excited and nervous at the same time. Associate Pastor?! Lord, have mercy! That weekend God led me to the story of David. I read 1 Samuel 16. In that chapter, David was in the field minding his own business, tending to his father's sheep when Samuel invited Jesse and his sons to the sacrifice where he consecrated Jesse and his sons. However, David was not present. After looking at all of Jesse's sons, Samuel asked, "Are these all your sons you have?" Jesse answered, "There is still the youngest. He is tending the sheep." Samuel said, "Send for him..." Once David arrived, the Lord said, "Rise and anoint him; this is the one." David was chosen above his brothers to be God's servant. David was working in the field and not part of the process when Samuel arrived to select one of Jesse's sons.

At the time, I had no idea why God had me read that story. Eventually, it would be revealed. The following Friday, I met with the District Superintendent and Pastor Haskins at a diner in East Baltimore to talk about the Associate Pastor's positions. This was the first time I met Pastor Haskins in an official capacity. Days later, I would meet with Pastor Haskins and the leaders of the church we would together serve. The day I showed up to meet with the leaders, Pastor Haskins met me in the parking lot and said, "I want you to know before you enter the meeting that someone else was chosen for this position. However, it did not work out, but you are the person for the job." Immediately I thought, "OKAY GOD." Reading the story of David, God prepared me for what he said. He later shared with me that when I met with him and the District Superintendent for the first time, God told him before I even spoke aloud that I was the one. God had a divine appointment. I thank God that I was chosen for "such a time as this."

3

YOU GOT THIS PRIOLEAU!

"As iron sharpens iron,
so one person sharpens another." Proverbs 27:17 (NIV)

We had no idea what God had in store for us serving together. Not sure of the road that we would travel together, Pastor Haskins encouraged me to lead from the beginning. He was not afraid to let my light shine. He would push me into greater. Whenever I appeared to be unsure of myself, he would say, "You got this, Prioleau." I remember the first funeral I had the opportunity to officiate at the church by myself. He called me the day of the funeral and said, "I forgot to ask you, had you ever officiated a funeral before? I know it's too late, but you got this, Prioleau." He was always encouraging and pushing me forward. I remember one day we introduced ourselves to a meeting full of clergy. He said, "My name is Bruce Haskins, and I am her associate pastor." We laughed, but that was his way of encouraging me. He wanted me to own my position as a pastor. He insisted that the church call me Pastor Prioleau and not Minister Prioleau. He wanted them to know that we shared the pastoral ministry. He became my pastor, mentor, and friend. I learned so much about leadership from serving with him. I learned the meaning of collaborative leadership. Coming from a background of top-down leadership, he taught me that leadership is a group effort. He taught me that leadership is best done together and not alone. There are still times when I need that reminder, but God is gracious enough to allow me to learn from my mistakes. He taught me to love God's people with unconditional love. He had a love for God's people and loved everyone equally and without partiality. I learned that ministry is ministry, and it must be done. He would say, "Ministry is ministry, Prioleau. We have to do it." I learned the importance of family first before ministry. Our first Sunday at the church, referring to his wife, he told the congregation, "You see that smile on that lady's face? I put that there, and I intend for it to stay there." He stressed marriage before ministry. Before we started serving together, he felt it was important that our spouses meet each other. He arranged for the four of us to meet in May of that year before we started serving that July. We prayed together for our families, our marriages, and our children. Ministry with him was so grace-filled. He allowed me to make mistakes, and sometimes we even laughed at them. One thing I would never forget about him was his love for "all things church." He loved the church and all things about the church. He had a love for God's Word. It was not strange for him to telephone me and say, "Prioleau, what are you doing? Let me share with you what I am reading." He studied God's Word daily and challenged me in my study. He would challenge me in my sermon preparation. He telephoned me one day and said, "How long does it take you to prepare a sermon? Remember, Prioleau, studying God's Word is your number one priority. Let the people do the work." He emphasized Ephesians 4 and reminded me that we are to "equip the people," and not do the work for them.

I had no idea why he called me that day, but I understood later that it was his way of teaching me. We shared the preaching ministry. He preached two Sundays a month, and I preached two Sundays a month. I would say to him, "You need to preach more. The people need to hear your voice." He would say, "It's okay; you got this, Prioleau." He pushed me to think on my own as a pastor and to trust my voice. If I asked him what he thought about something, he would reply, "I am not thinking, you are thinking. Now tell me what you are thinking?" We dreamed and planned together for the church. We would talk about our plans for the church and where we saw God in the life of the church. We would talk about where God was calling the church in that season. From what he said and did not say, he taught me how to be a pastor. We were leading, and he was leading by example. There are some things seminary will teach you, but there are some things that are taught only by living through it. During our time in ministry together, God was gracious to me. God gave me the strength and grace to do ministry in a rewarding way. We launched new ministries and cast vision together. A church richly blessed with an abundance of persons called to set apart ministry, we started a ministry team with those retired pastors, certified candidates for ordained ministry, and certified lay ministers. He desired that leaders lead to their fullest potential. There are times when I can still hear him saying, "You got this, Prioleau!" It was my first-time pastoring, and it grew me up in ministry fast. I am sure I have a lot to learn, but those years fast-tracked me into ministry. Baptism into ministry by fire is what I call it. I believe I am the pastor I am today because of his leadership. God used Pastor Haskins to teach me lessons that I could glean from for a lifetime. Sometimes we don't get it right away, but as time goes on, God will bring things back to our remembrance. As the hymn writer said, "We will understand it better by and by." Serving with Pastor Haskins was such a blessing. We served wonderfully together, and I thank God for the opportunity to have served with him. He was a pastor's pastor.

4
DEEP WATERS

"But Jesus immediately said to them: "Take courage! It is I. Don't be afraid." "Lord, if it's you," Peter replied, "tell me to come to you on the water." "Come," he said. Then Peter got down out of the boat, walked on the water, and came toward Jesus. But when he saw the wind, he was afraid and, beginning to sink, cried out, "Lord, save me!"
Matthew 14:27-30

One day ministry would change for us. Pastor Haskins had health challenges that had an impact on the ministry and would play a pivotal role in our time together. Actually, it ended up shaping our time together. In May 2013, Pastor Haskins' son died tragically due to violence on the streets of Baltimore City. Pastor Haskins looked to me for leadership. Our roles would change. I walked him and his family through the process of burying their loved one. Then it happened again. Over a year later, in November 2014, his nephew died tragically due to violence on the streets of Baltimore County.

I believe grief has an impact on the heart. I think grief breaks that heart. Quoted from his wife, Dr. Deborah Haskins, "Murder murders the heart." After the death of his son and nephew, his already fragile heart began to fail. First, from a broken heart and then physical, he was moving slower than usual. I could tell that Pastor Haskins was slowing down. He had a history of heart attacks. In the past, Pastor Haskins had two major surgeries before suffering three heart attacks in one week. He shared how God healed him, as that was his testimony. However, grief was taking a toll on his heart. Hospital visits were frequent. He shared with me that he was slowing down and did not have the energy he used to have.

The reality of the situation was, because of his condition, I had to always be "ON"- On meaning, I had to continually be ready for what the day had to offer us. Pastoring was full of unforeseen emergencies. It seemed like daily I was called upon to deal with the death of members of the congregation as well as crises surrounding the senior pastor's health. We were serving an aging yet vibrant membership, and quite a few members passed away during our time there. I had to be ready at all times. It seemed like I had no days off. I would forgo vacation or arrange vacation around the health of the senior pastor. However, he was still serving and serving to the best of his ability. Pastor Haskins had an unwavering love for the ministry and the Lord.

At the beginning of 2015, Pastor Haskins and I launched the theme "Launching Out into the Deep." We had no idea the deep waters we would find ourselves in that year as pastors and as a congregation. In January of that year, my 101-year-old grandmother passed away, and in February, Pastor Haskins' health took a turn for the worst. He was hospitalized most of the year.

Trying to grieve the loss of my grandmother, I had to pastor the congregation and be the pastor to the pastor and his family. My role changed, and I now became the pastor of the pastor. I was thrust into leading the congregation. It was a very trying time for all of us, but as I reflect, it was also a time full of God's grace. God gave me the grace needed to lead during that time. Was it always perfect? No! But that's what so amazing about grace. Grace meets you at your lowest. Grace grabs you when you feel like you want to let go. Grace covers you in all of your imperfections. Grace is taking our faults and mixing it with God's unconditional love to bring forth God's plan. God gave me the wisdom to seek the help of a professional coach and colleagues to help talk me through tough decisions.

I had to make decisions I had not encountered before. I was in deep waters. I no longer had the Senior Pastor to talk me through the challenges I was facing. I was now preaching every Sunday. There were times when I visited him, and I wished I could ask him his opinion and how he thought I should handle a situation. I needed his wisdom, but I knew he could not lead from a hospital bed. He would ask how the church was, and I would reply, "Everything is okay." I could not tell him that we were struggling. I could not say to him that the members were anxious and concerned about his well-being. They were genuinely worried about their pastor. I could not tell him that I felt like I was in deep waters over my head. My heart was hurting, and I felt like I could not share it with anyone. I felt like I had to put my feelings on the back burner and keep leading. I felt like everything depended on my leadership. There were times when I felt like I had it together, but there were times when it felt like everything was pulled from under me. I remember waking up one morning with a headache. As I prepared myself for the day, the headache got worse and worse. I thought I would be okay, but as I put my coat on, I felt like I had to vomit. I went into the bathroom and grew weak. I called my husband, who was already at work, and told him I needed to go to the emergency room. He took me to the emergency room, and they told me I was suffering from a migraine. They gave me medication, and I rested at home for a few days.

I knew God was with me, but I had many lonely moments. I felt like I was leading alone. We had launched out into deep waters. We had no idea of how we would live into that when we cast that vision. Some of the decisions I made during that time were not good ones, but I thank God for grace. Some of the members were upset with me for some of the decisions I made. Some even stopped attending worship for a period of time. Ministry seemed to stand still. Sometimes I could not make decisions fast enough. I was carrying a heavy burden. I shouldered the burdens/cares of the congregation while holding the pastor and his family close to my heart.

Nehemiah 4:10 says, "But Judah said, 'The strength of the burden bearers is failing, and there is too much rubbish so that we are unable to work on the wall.'" In Nehemiah, so much was happening around the people that were building the wall that their strength began to fail. The naysayers were taunting them. So much was coming up against them as they tried to rebuild; conflict from within and without. Nehemiah had to step in and encourage their hearts. He told them to remember why they were rebuilding. Sometimes the burden of ministry can be so great, and we must remind ourselves of why we said, "Yes" to the call in the first place.

I knew I had to do something to assure the congregation that God was with us even if I felt like I was drowning. I called my coach, and she helped me process how a meeting would look with the leaders. One Saturday, I called the leadership together and said, "When Pastor Haskins and I launched the theme of 'Launching Out into the Deep,' we had no idea how it would manifest itself. However, we all can agree that we are in deep waters. God has called us into deep waters. We need to trust that God is with us in deep waters." That day we cried and prayed together. I prayed for the leaders, and the leaders prayed for me. I had no idea how that year would turn out. All I knew was that we were in deep waters, and I needed to trust God while treading.

All of this took place during the year that Baltimore experienced uprising around the death of Freddie Gray. We were serving in one of the communities that experienced the riots. Our congregation was one of the United Methodist Churches in Baltimore City that was on the front line during that time. We attended meetings and strategized on how we could meet the needs of that community. That was a challenging time in the history of Baltimore, and the church was showing up. The riots left some people depleted of necessary resources. Our church became a drop-off center for supplies donated by churches from throughout the Baltimore-Washington Conference. We launched a summer camp to give neighborhood children a safe place to go. In one month, we planned a six-week summer camp that would run simultaneously in three locations. Each location served roughly 50 neighborhood children. On the last day of the camp session, I got sick. We took the children to the park, and I would spend the entire time in my car with a temperature. I left the park, returned to the church, and fell asleep in the office until I had the strength to go home.

5

NOT NOW

"A waiting person is a patient person. The word patience means the willingness to stay where we are and live the situation out to the full in the belief that something hidden there will manifest itself to us."
— *Henri J.M. Nouwen*

In addition to dealing with ministry struggles, I had personal struggles. All of this happened while I was due to go before the Board of Ordained Ministry in hopes of being approved to be ordained as an Elder in Full Connection in the United Methodist Church. When it was my time to appear before the board, things did not go well. My head was not in the game. My mind was all over the place. I arrived to the exam, and by lunchtime, I had an excruciating headache. Reflecting, showing up was all that I did. I was not mentally prepared for the exam. That year I was not approved to be ordained as an Elder in Full Connection in the United Methodist Church.

Hearing the words, "you were not approved," broke my heart. It was as if time stood still. I cried. But one of my mentors reminded me, "God is in control of your destiny."

When I called her that morning, she said, "Twanda, what is the worst that could happen?" I had to think about it. My reply, "that I have to go before the Board next year." She replied, "Okay, prepare for next year. You did not hear, "No." You heard, "Not Now." God has a perfect plan in place for our lives. Sometimes we put a period where God has placed a comma. For me, it was as if that chapter had ended, but it did not. I needed to turn the page. God has a process for our lives, and we need to trust God's process. God's plan was for me at that time was "not now."

Then a change happened. On September 13, 2015, it was announced to the congregation that Pastor Haskins and I would be leaving the church as of October 15, 2015, and they would be receiving a new Senior Pastor. I had been appointed to serve as the new Senior Pastor of Christ United Methodist Church. I was excited about the new opportunity, but I also had many mixed emotions. So many questions flooded my mind. What is it like at the new congregation? Am I ready? How would they receive me? How would I be as a senior pastor? These were legitimate questions in my mind. It was time for me to leave the church I had served over the past four years. This is the moment where it all started. I was torn. My heart was with this congregation, Pastor Haskins and his family. Also, a pastoral transition typically happens on July 1 in the United Methodist Church. While situations necessitate a transition at other times throughout the calendar year, it's rare. I was moving to another appointment outside of the appointment season, but we, the congregation and myself, needed to trust God's plan. God was taking me through a process, and I had to trust God's process.

The day it was announced that I was leaving, I preached a sermon entitled "Trust God in the Process." God took me back to that camel ride in seminary. I preached to the congregation, and I preached to myself. Life is a process, and we are encouraged to trust God as we go through life's process. Proverbs 3:5 states, "Trust in the LORD with all your heart and lean not on your own understanding; in all your ways submit to him, and he will make your paths straight." (NIV) Trust does not come easy, and it's not easy to practice when you are amid life's challenges, but it's what we are called to do as Christians.

I believe our mind is programmed to trust what we understand only, and that's why the Bible calls for us to renew our minds. For most of us, if we don't understand all the details, we won't do it. If we don't fully comprehend the plan of God, most of us won't follow God. If we don't understand where God is taking us, we won't go. This text pushed me and challenged me to lean not to my own understanding. There are going to be somethings in the plan of God that I will never understand. But God is calling me to trust God in the process. Most of the time, God does not reveal the entire plan to us. Who would have known that the senior pastor would get sick during our time serving together? Who would have known that I would be leading that congregation by myself? Who would have known God would call us to these deep waters? However, I have learned that we don't need to see the whole plan; we just need to know the God who has the plan. All I need to understand is God's mercy, grace, faithfulness, kindness, righteousness, power, and justice is with me. "TRUST GOD IN THE PROCESS."

6

LEADING ON "E"

"Restore to me the joy of your salvation and grant me a willing spirit, to sustain me." Psalm 51:12 (NIV)

As I moved into this new position as a senior pastor, I was still pastoring Pastor Haskins and his family. I thank God for the opportunity to journey with him and his family through his illness. It was a humbling experience. Here I am in my first lead pastor position, still young in ministry, and I am walking this seasoned pastor and his family through what would be one of the most challenging times of their lives. In January of 2016, just two months into my new appointment, Pastor Haskins passed away. I was there with his family when he took his last breath. The grace in that room was unbelievable and evident. With one of his favorite songs, "Take Me to The King" sung by Tamela Mann, playing in the background, surrounded by his family, with his wife ushering him into the presence of the Lord, Pastor Haskins passed away. Selah. That day in the hospital, one of my colleagues looked at me and said, "You need to take time to process things." At that moment, with so much going on, I did not fully understand his words. I walked Pastor Haskins' family through the process of planning his Homegoing service and was back in the pulpit preaching the following Sunday. I was leading a new congregation. I had only been there two months. So, I carried on with business as usual.

However, what I did not realize was that I was empty. I was tired. I needed to take time to BREATHE! In the process of leading, I did not refill my cup. In the process of giving, I had given my all. My cup was no longer overflowing; it was empty. I had nothing left in my cup. I had lost my grandmother AND a pastor-mentor-colleague-friend. I did not allow myself to voice how I was feeling or allow myself to feel the impact of what was happening during that time. I did not allow myself time to cry or hurt. My thoughts were, "Who was I to hurt? This family lost a loved one. Why am I feeling sad?"

A couple of months after Pastor Haskins' passing, a dear friend, Mrs. Somerville, suddenly died. Mrs. Somerville was my friend and confidant. She was the one I could go to and share some of my deepest fears. She would listen deeply. I could cry on this lady's lap. I could talk to her, and she would know by the sound of my voice that I was troubled. Our conversations often went like this.

Mrs. Somerville: How are you?

Me: Fine.

Mrs. Somerville: Make me believe you.

She knew when things were not right. As I reflect, I went through the same emotions when she passed. I walked her family through the process of planning her Homegoing service. I did not allow myself to feel the pain of her death. I ministered and helped her family go through the process of burying their loved one, and then I went back to ministry as usual. I did not take a Sunday away from my responsibilities. I kept going. As I reflect, I had not allowed myself to grieve. I did not grieve my grandmother's death; I did not grieve Pastor Haskins' death, and I did not grieve Mrs. Somerville's death. I kept leading, but now I was going along with the motions of ministry, but not the fulfillment of ministry. Ministry was no longer fulfilling to me. In May 2018, I realized I had had enough.

7
ENOUGH

... while he himself went a day's journey into the wilderness. He came to a broom bush, sat down under it and prayed that he might die. "I have had enough... 1 Kings 19:4 (NIV)

You ever wake up one morning, and for some reason, you don't feel like yourself anymore? You feel like you lost something deep inside of yourself. You can't pinpoint it. You're not sure when you lost it. You don't understand what it is, but you know that something is gone. That "IT" that you had is not there anymore. You don't know what is missing, but you know whatever "IT" is, it has left you.

That's what I felt as I moved towards burnout. I knew that something was gone, but I could not pinpoint it. I could not focus. I had lost my zeal for ministry. It did not seem like I had the creativity for the ministry I once had. It was gone, and I was not quite sure what happened. I tried everything I could to bring "IT" back. Maybe I should attend another conference. Maybe I should attend a workshop. Maybe I need another week of vacation. Maybe I need to connect with another clergy. Maybe I need a couple days off. Perhaps

I am just not cut out for this thing called "pastoring." I started questioning my reason for being a pastor.

Maybe I need to find a job doing something else. I have an accounting degree; perhaps I can work as an accountant. My husband owns his own business; maybe I can find something to do with him. Perhaps it's the church I am serving. Maybe I need to strategize more with my leadership. Maybe I need a change of appointment. Perhaps my time serving this congregation was up. I thought about many things I could do to bring my "IT" back. I even thought about submitting my letter of resignation. Yes, that crossed my mind. I did not have "IT" for this anymore. I had suffered from anxiety and depression in the past, and I was afraid it was resurfacing. I have been down that road before, and I know what it feels like to be in a dark place. I thought, "God, I don't want to revisit that time in my life again." However, something was wrong, and I did not know what "IT" was. I knew that I needed to make a change, but I did not understand what I needed to change. I knew that I needed to stop, but I did not know how to stop.

In July 2017, after talking with a mentor and from her recommendation, I made an appointment with a therapist. On the first day, I got a reality check. As I prepared to leave my home, I received a call that one of my members was rushed to the hospital. I decided I would keep my appointment and visit the member once I finished. That day the therapist shared with me, "Don't forsake yourself during it all. You believe that ministry is about self-sacrifice. However, you cannot sacrifice self if you don't have a self to give." The therapist's words hit me like a ton of bricks. I had never heard self-sacrifice described in that way.

"You can't sacrifice self if you don't have a self to give." I left my appointment and went to visit my member in the emergency room. However, during that hospital visit, I began to feel sick. I wasn't sure what was happening, but I was getting weaker in my body. The more I sat there, the worse I felt. I did not want to share with the family that I was not feeling well. In my mind, I was thinking, "This is not good; I need to leave." I decided to have prayer with family and ended the visit. However, as I was praying, I got so weak I felt like I was about to pass out. I sat back down and shared with them that I was not feeling well. They asked if I needed the doctor, and I declined. I drank some water, sat there for about five minutes, and then went out to the waiting area. This episode resulted in an overnight stay in the hospital from exhaustion and dehydration.

After the incident in the hospital, another seasoned pastor and mentor called me and said, "Twanda, God did not give you a platter. You are trying to lead from a platter. God only gave you a cup and a saucer. You need to decide what you need to give up and concentrate on one thing." Her words hit me like a ton of bricks. It was time for me to slow down, but I did not know how. I did not know what I could take off my plate, and I did not realize the burden I was carrying. As I reflect, I now know it was much more than removing things from my plate. It was about learning how to balance my life as a pastor. It was about me not getting lost in the process of tending to the souls of others. It was about trusting God in the process. It was more than removing things off my plate.

However, I kept going. I kept leading, but now I was going along with the motions of ministry and not the fulfillment of ministry. Ministry was no longer fulfilling to me.

Around midnight on Friday, May 5, 2018, ten months later, came the breaking point. I was in Pittsburgh, Pennsylvania at a training. I was still up, talking to the colleague with whom I was sharing a room. We were talking about the challenges of ministry. I was sitting on my bed, surrounded by my schoolbooks, working on an overdue paper. At the time, I was in a Doctor of Ministry program at United Theological Seminary. That night, during our conversation, I began to feel anxious and overwhelmed. I knew I needed to do something to change how I had been feeling. The days leading up to our trip to Pittsburgh, my schedule was overbooked. I had attended a three-day retreat that ended on Wednesday, and I had to be in Pittsburgh on Thursday. The retreat was called "Tending the Fire," a retreat that taught leaders how to be a non-anxious presence. At that retreat, I had to ask myself, "Am I an anxious presence in the congregation?" I could identify with many of the things we discussed. My schedule was managing me. I was not managing my schedule. My schedule was overbooked, and it was overwhelming.

I knew I had overextended myself and tried to find ways to get out of attending this training in Pittsburgh. I was four hours away from home. So many things were going through my mind. The training did not end until Sunday morning, and I needed to be back in Baltimore on Sunday morning to preach. How was I going to finish this paper? I could not concentrate. I remember thinking, "I need to slow down." My colleague had no idea I was dealing with this as we talked. Our conversation brought to me the realization that I was not in a good place. I felt like I was about to have a panic attack. The room felt like it was getting smaller and smaller. I felt closed in. I needed air. Maybe I should take a walk. I remember thinking, "This is not good."

My colleague shared with me that she was taking a sabbath leave that summer and asked if I had considered taking one. I started counting the years I had served in ministry and whether I qualified for a sabbath leave. In the Baltimore-Washington Conference, the conference in which I serve, a clergy person serving full-time can take a three-month sabbath leave every seven years. As I pondered her question, even the thought of taking off was overwhelming. I closed my books and went to bed. I could not sleep. Floods of emotions were going through my head. I prayed all night long. "Lord, calm my anxious spirit. God, I am empty. Lord, I need a break. God, I can't go on like this any longer." All night, tears rolled down my eyes. I felt like I had hit a brick wall. I had given ministry all that I had. I had reached my breaking point.

Early the next morning, around 7 a.m., with tears in my eyes, I called my husband and shared with him that I was considering taking a sabbath leave. At the same time, I texted my district superintendent and asked her could she give me a call at her earliest convenience. In the United Methodist Church, District Superintendents serve in a supervisory position over a geographic area. With tears in my eyes, I shared with her that I was overwhelmed and needed to "tap out." I had reached my breaking point. I thank God for her care and pastoral leadership during that conversation. I then called the necessary leadership in my church to start the process of taking a three-month sabbath leave. I called one of my colleagues to ask her if she would preach for me that Sunday morning, and she said, "Yes." I was exhausted, and I had nothing left to give.

That Sunday morning, God confirmed through the preached Word the decision to take a sabbath leave. Not knowing the challenges I was facing, my colleague preached on Elijah under the Juniper tree. Her sermon was entitled, "It Ain't Over," from 1 Kings 19:1- 8 (NIV).

"Now Ahab told Jezebel everything Elijah had done and how he had killed all the prophets with the sword. So Jezebel sent a messenger to Elijah to say, "May the gods deal with me, be it ever so severely if by this time tomorrow I do not make your life like that of one of them." Elijah was afraid and ran for his life. When he came to Beersheba in Judah, he left his servant there, while he went a day's journey into the wilderness. He came to a broom bush, sat down under it and prayed that he might die. **"I have had enough, Lord," he said**. "Take my life; I am no better than my ancestors." Then he lay down under the bush and fell asleep. All at once, an angel touched him and said, "Get up and eat." He looked around, and there by his head was some bread baked over hot coals and a jar of water. He ate and drank and then lay down again. The angel of the Lord came back a second time and touched him and said, "Get up and eat, for the journey is too much for you." So, he got up and ate and drank. Strengthened by that food, he traveled forty days and forty nights until he reached Horeb, the mountain of God."

Tears rolled down my face as she began to preach. She said,

> "I've yet to meet someone who's never felt like giving up. I've yet to encounter the person who has never wanted or never wished that life came with a RESET button. We make mistakes/errors in judgment and feel as if we're the first person who has ever failed. Life happens, and we're shaken. Things occur that we can't control. Jobs close. The economy tanks. The market is unstable. Friends fail. And even though we can't control what occurs, what occurs tries to control us. There are people in this sanctuary

right now who are facing scenarios we never thought we'd have to deal with, and if we let our emotions get the best of us, we'll give in, give up and declare that it's over." The Reverend Antionette Gatewood-Sykes

God had a Word just for me. That Word spoke to me in a deeply personal way. It spoke to the depths of my soul. I cried during worship. As I sat there and listened to that sermon, I had to admit ministry had taken a toll on me. I was not taking care of myself as much as I should have. I was not bringing my best self to ministry. I was tired. My zeal was gone. It felt like I was not hearing from God clear anymore. I had given ministry all that I had stored up in me, and I had nothing else to offer. I was in my seventh year of pastoral ministry, and it was draining me. I had to admit, "I've had enough."

Two weeks later, the clergy of the Baltimore Metropolitan District assembled for our quarterly clergy gathering. During our time together, our District Superintendent gifted each of us with a resurrection plant. A resurrection plant is a plant whose name is derived "from its habit of drying up and turning brown in the summer and fall, and then 'resurrecting' when exposed to rainfall in winter and spring." It was given to remind us of God's ability to resurrect whatever dry places we experience in our ministries. When I received that plant, God again affirmed my decision to take sabbath leave. It was the Lord's doing! That plant reminded me that there are seasons in our lives when we dry up and need to be RESURRECTED. However, we are best resurrected when we are exposed to the rain of God's Spirit. Resurrection happens when we separate ourselves from the busyness of everyday life, spend time with God, and allow God to speak to the dry places in our lives. As clergy, it's hard for us to

BREATHE!

separate ourselves from the busyness of ministry. Ministry happens all the time, and the repetitiveness of it can lead us into a dry place. I was in a dry place and needed to learn how to BREATHE. **It was now time to BREATHE.**

8
BREATHE

"But Jesus often withdrew to lonely places and prayed."
Luke 5:16

Sabbath leave was a time for me to step back and
BREATHE! What did I do during this time? I stepped
back from those things that were pulling on the very essence
of my soul and spent time connecting to the things in my life
that feed into my spirit in new ways. I had the opportunity to
reflect on the last seven years of pastoral ministry. I wrote a
lot. I took a three-day personal retreat. I exercised. I listened
to my body. Life slowed down for me. I connected with my
family in new ways. The first relationship that suffers is the
family. The demand of ministry sometimes pulls us away
from our families. As a result, we disconnect in so many
ways, which can inevitably lead to pastors living isolated
from the ones we love. We sometimes miss birthdays and
important events in the lives of our loved ones because it
conflicts with ministry obligations. I had to step back and
find that balance between family and ministry. Stepping
back was a sign of throwing up my hands and surrendering
myself, my family, and my ministry to God. It was the best

way I could tell God, "I give up. I cannot do this in my own strength anymore." I had to disconnect to connect.

First, I did nothing. I disconnected. I had absolutely no agenda. Disconnecting was learning when to say, "no." I disconnected from the work of the church. I had things in place so that even in case of an emergency, the church would not call me. I want you to understand that deciding to take a sabbath leave was not easy. Like many, we wondered if the church would survive the pastor being away for three months. It's the reality of ministry. However, I had to disconnect from that type of thinking. I canceled all my previously booked engagements for those three months. Canceling outside commitments was not an easy decision. I prayed that they would understand. I disconnected from those things in my life that were pulling on me, and some of the pull I was experiencing was the expectation of ministry I placed on myself. I needed to let that go.

I had to understand that everybody's emergency did not have to be my emergency. I pushed back on running towards other people's problems and faced the struggles that were going on in my own life. I had some things I needed to deal with that were draining me. I needed to take other people's problems to God and not try to fix it myself. I am naturally a fix-it person. When I face a challenge, I automatically feel a need to fix it or find a solution. I needed to push back from that. I pushed back on thinking I needed to be everyone's savior. I had to be intentional about pushing back. I had to purpose in my mind to say, "No." It hurt at first because I was saying "no" to places where I wanted to show up, but I knew that I had to separate myself. I started giving me attention.

The only thing I placed on my calendar for three months was me. I had to be selfish with my time for a season if I was to heal. I had to give myself the grace I naturally gave others by showing up for myself. I started looking at those areas in my life that I needed to give attention to. It became a time of self-discovery because I had lost me amidst everything. I know we are called to a ministry of self-sacrifice, but as my therapist said, "You can't give self if you don't have a self to give." I needed to find myself.

Second, I connected. Three days of the week, I would meet my exercise group at 5:30 a.m. to workout. On the other days, I would get up and sit in my sunroom. Eventually, I formed a habit of waking up and meeting God. It was either during my ride to work out or in my sunroom; I was spending time with God. It became my quiet time, something I was no longer doing because I allowed the busyness of ministry to push it out. I started reading books that spoke to my soul. I read *Love is An Inside Job* by Romal Tune and *The Emotionally Healthy Leader* by Peter Scazzero. Both were stories of personal triumph. In Romal's book, he shares his story of how he found healing through therapy. What I loved most about this book is the authenticity in which it was written. He was open about his past and how it impacted his life. In Peter's book, he speaks to the busyness of ministry and how we can push out the things that matter to us the most when ministry becomes number one in our lives. Real transformation in our church happens when we are transformed on the inside. We must remember, "who you are is more important than what you do." I could identify with his struggle as a pastor allowing the ministry to push family in the background. I highly recommend both books. They both helped to restore my soul and reconnect me to God and family in a healthy way. God used them to minister to my soul.

BREATHE!

I connected with my therapist and started seeing her weekly. These sessions allowed me to reflect on the past seven years of ministry in a healthy way. The question with which I struggled during that time was, what is it about me that I feel the need to overwork myself and be present for everyone? Together, we worked out a plan for when I returned to the parish. How would my time look? What will I change so that I do not find myself back in this place where I have to take sabbath leave? She told me, "The beauty of integrating back into life, you get to choose where you want your energy to go."

I connected with God. I planned a retreat of solitude. I separated to listen for God's still small voice. Interestingly, busyness can drown out the voice of God. When we slow down, we hear God speak in a new and refreshing way. I went to Sandy Cove Ministries for three days. Sandy Cove is a retreat center in North East, Maryland, on the Chesapeake Bay. They offer mini sabbaticals for ministry leaders at a minimum cost. You arrive on a Monday and leave Wednesday. All meals included. I love that they have no televisions on-site. Therefore, I was not tempted to simply go to my room and watch television all day. I spent that time alone with God. Looking back, God was waiting for me there. God was waiting for that moment. I found a tree that faces the water, and I sat under that tree every day. In three days, I fell in love with that tree. That tree became a place of healing for me. I cried under that tree. I grieved under that tree. I grieved people I had lost over the last few years. I grieved my grandmother. I grieved Pastor Haskins. I grieved Mrs. Somerville. But I also smiled under that tree. It was a place where I found peace. It was a place that allowed me to let go and just be. It was a place where I connected with God. It was a place where I could breathe. I had an opportunity to reflect on ministry. Most of what I wrote in this book, I wrote under that tree. My mind was clear. I felt light. No longer did I feel like I was carrying the cares of the world. It was under that tree that I learned to BREATHE!

EPILOGUE

"We all are hearing the words, 'I can't breathe' across our nation, but it's important that we step back and take the time to breathe so that we are there to stand up for those who have lost their breath."
— *Twanda Prioleau*

As I finish this book, I am now two years removed from my sabbath leave, and our nation is in a cultural shift. We are currently experiencing a global pandemic. We are experiencing civil unrest and fighting racial inequality. Pastors are now in overdrive. However, I must encourage my colleagues to find time to step back and breathe. You must care for your soul. Over the last two years, I have learned that we must find ways to step away from ministry. It is not an option. Clergy burnout is real.

Seeking healing and wholeness for myself, I am now pursuing a master's degree in Mental Health Counseling. It is my desire to help pastors balance the waters of ministry. As I stated earlier in this book, I was enrolled in United Theological Seminary, pursuing a Doctor of Ministry as a Rev. Dr. Martin Luther King, Jr. scholar. After taking three months off, I dropped out of the program. I felt God leading me in another direction. As I sought healing from clergy burnout, I wondered how many pastors feel the same as I did. Maybe I can be a blessing to other pastors.

BREATHE!

Currently, I focus a lot on self-care. Caring for myself amid ministry is not an option. Daily I seek balance. It's not easy. Therefore, you must purposely and intentionally find ways to bring rest into your life. It is vital that we take care of ourselves. Our whole self. Not just the outside, but the inside. Not just the inside, but the outside. It is only through caring for our own souls that we can authentically care for others. Shelly Miller, in her book *Rhythms of Rest – Finding the Spirit of Sabbath in a Busy World*, talks about dispelling the legalistic idea about the sabbath, the idea of seeing sabbath as a day of rest. She talks about finding time to rest, whether for an hour, a morning, or a whole day can change your perspective about the way we approach life.

I believe too often we view sabbath as an event on our calendar. While our calendars remind us of sabbath, we cannot wait until the scheduled day to come to choose to rest. We must find sabbath daily. I call it "sabbathing." Find ways each day to bring sabbath into your life. Find ways to step back daily, even if it is no more than getting up from your desk and taking a 10-minute walk by yourself to breathe. Stop in the middle of your day, put on one of your favorite songs, and dance by yourself. Stop at a park on the drive home, and take a ten-minute walk. Do breathing exercises throughout your day. You must take time to breathe in the midst of it all. Place you on your calendar. Block off time in your schedule for you. Mark the words "I'm busy" throughout your calendar and do not negotiate that time. You must manage your calendar and not allow your calendar to manage you.

I know it might be hard using that word "Breathe" at a time when we all are hearing the words "I can't breathe," ring out across the American nation, but it's important that we step back and take the time to breathe so that we are there to stand up for those who have lost their breath. We must take care of ourselves and **BREATHE.**

BREATHE!

The next few pages are full of journal entries I wrote during my sabbath leave. It was in the silence of those moments that I had an opportunity to reflect. I invite you to use these pages as your journal. In these pages, I share what I learned during that time. After each reflection is a blank page. Use the black pages to write your reflections and where you are in this season of life. Maybe God is calling you to BREATHE! *"But Jesus often withdrew to lonely places and prayed."* Luke: 5:16

SABBATH REFLECTION I

"but whoever drinks the water I give them will never thirst. Indeed, the water I give them will become in them a spring of water welling up to eternal life."
John 4:14 (NIV)

If we are not careful, we can find ourselves leading out of an empty cup. The only way our cup can be overflowing is we have to have that cup refilled continuously. The more you drink or allow someone else to drink out of your cup without refilling it, the less you have in that cup. You must allow yourself to be refilled. We can't give what we don't have. I had nothing left to give. My calendar was guiding me; I was no longer guiding my calendar. I felt guilty if I had a day with nothing to do. I felt guilty if I had to cancel a meeting because I was tired or sick. So, I showed up fatigued or ill. I was not caring for myself. I moved until I had to stop, then I was back in the race again. Are you leading out of an empty cup? Pray that God will lead you to a well; a well that is overflowing with water for you to drink from.

SABBATH REFLECTION II

*"The Lord is close to the brokenhearted and saves those who are
crushed in spirit. The righteous person may have many troubles, but
the Lord delivers him from them all;"*
Psalm 34:18-19 (NIV)

God has called us into this great ministry, and we would
not quit if we could. It's just that great of a call.
However, I believe in tending to God's flock, God has called
us to also tend to our own souls. We must take the time to
step back and allow God to nourish us during it all. It is only
when the soul can breathe does it open itself for healing.
What places in your life do you need to seek God for
healing?

SABBATH REFLECTION III

"Do you not know that your bodies are temples of the Holy Spirit, who is in you, whom you have received from God? You are not your own; you were bought at a price. Therefore, honor God with your bodies
1 Corinthians 6:19-20

It might not be everyone's plight, but I am sure some can identify with the wear and tear of ministry. I realized that over the past seven years, I have not been taking care of myself. I gained 30 lbs. over the past seven years of ministry. Although I was not dealing with any health issues, gaining weight was a sign of self-neglect. Before I became a full-time pastor, I ran. I ran two half-marathons the year I started my first appointment. After that, the ministry became an excuse for me not to tend to me. I was too tired. I got home too late. I had an early morning meeting. I had so many excuses. As a result, I was not in a good place. Taking care of the body is just as important as anything else in our lives. When was the last time you gave attention to your physical well-being?

SABBATH REFLECTION IV

"Do not conform to the pattern of this world but be transformed by the renewing of your mind. Then you will be able to test and approve what God's will is – his good, pleasing, and perfect.
Romans 12:2 NIV

R echarging the mind is essential. We must step back and allow God to renew our minds daily. We participate in and engage so many conversations throughout our day, and that day to day interaction can fill our minds with things that wear us down mentally. Daily communication with God allows us to renew our minds. As pastors, it's vital that we not only investigate God's Word for a sermon but to allow God to speak directly to our spirit that we may be renewed daily. Pastoring takes a lot out of us, and many pastors don't take the rest we need. Many of us don't step back. Because of that, we lead on empty. Sometimes we are just showing up and regurgitating sermons, no new revelation. We are operating off a platter when God only gave us a cup and saucer.

I tried to give what I did not have. I tried to minister on empty because I did not realize that I was empty. I did not know that I was leading on empty. Sometimes we don't realize that we don't have what we don't have. Sometimes we can keep going and not know that the "it" we had is gone. I knew that I was tired, but I did not realize how tired I was. I was going along with the motions of ministry, but not the fulfillment of ministry. What can you do today to renew your mind?

SABBATH REFLECTION V

"After he had dismissed them, he went up on a mountainside by himself to pray. Later that night, he was there alone,"
Matthew 14:23

As I reflect while on sabbath leave, one thing I have come to understand is that I really like being alone. As much as I love being around people, my soul was yearning to be alone. What feeds my soul more than being with others is being by myself. Take the time to be with yourself. Your self will thank you. Ministry is a crowded place, and crowds can block what's needed to feed the soul. Sometimes we must get into that quiet place. That place of rest. That place where you hear God. Get into that quiet place. Sabbath is not a one day a week event; it's an everyday occurrence. When was the last time you spent time alone with God?

SABBATH REFLECTION VI

"Therefore, do not worry about tomorrow, for tomorrow will worry about itself. Each day has enough trouble of its own." Matthew 6:34

As leaders, we can find ourselves in a place of always looking for our next. God what are you doing next; what is happening next; what do you want me to say next? We do not allow ourselves to sit in our now. Sometimes we must glean from what is happening now, and in the midst of now, what's happening next will just happen. We do not have to seek out our next; it will naturally happen. What is God currently doing in your life that you can learn from?

SABBATH REFLECTION VII

"Sing to the Lord a new song; sing to the Lord, all the earth. Sing to the Lord, praise his name; proclaim his salvation day after day. Psalm 96:1-2

Sometimes we dance to the same beat for so long that we forget that there are other sounds out there. Change your beat. What in your life do you need to change to allow space for you to slow down?

SABBATH REFLECTION VIII

"As the deer pants for streams of water,
so my soul pants for you, my God.
Psalm 42:1

In stepping back, I realized that what feeds my soul the most is not being with others but being by myself. During my sabbath leave, I awake every morning yearning to sit with myself. Ministry is a crowded place, and crowds can be a loud place. Crowds can drown out the sounds needed to feed your soul. Get into that quiet place, that place of rest. Get into the place where you hear God. Get into that place where you hear God, not for a sermon but for your own care. Get into that quiet place. Your self will thank you. I am learning that sabbath is not a one day a week event; it's an everyday occurrence. Sabbath leave has allowed me to get in that quiet place. The quiet place for me is not necessarily a physical place, but it's a place in my soul. A place in my soul that I had not tapped into for a long time. It's a place in my soul that was yearning to be heard, a place in my soul that needed attention. My soul has had an opportunity to settle and rest. Sometimes the cares of ministry can be so much that our soul is not allowed to be quiet. What is your

BREATHE!

heart yearning for as it pertains to your relationship with God?

Made in the USA
Coppell, TX
07 November 2020

40885773R00046